More Picturing Chinese

MORE PICTURING CHINESE

ThunderStone Books
Las Vegas, Nevada

Text © Thunderstone Books, 2016
Illustrations © Bennett Noorda, 2016

This book may not be reproduced in whole or in part, in any form or by any means, electronic or mechanical, including photocopying, recording, or by any information storage and retrieval system now known or hereafter invented, without written permission from the publisher.

978-1-63411-004-4 (ISBN 13)

About This Book

This book begins with an introduction to stroke order to provide six simple rules for writing Chinese. Just as English letters are to be written in a specific line order, each stroke of Chinese characters needs to be written in a particular order as well. Similar to its companion book, *Picturing Chinese*, this book has pictures to accompany twelve of the most common Chinese characters to help you create a repertoire of the building blocks of Chinese writing. Use these building blocks to better understand pieces of other, more complicated characters.

For additional tools to accompany this book and supplement your Chinese language learning, visit www.thunderstonebooks.com.

About Stroke Order

When writing Chinese characters, stroke order (or the order in which the different parts are written) is very important. Rather than learn the correct stroke order for each individual character, there are certain rules that make determining how to write each character fairly straightforward. It is important to learn these rules well when starting to write characters, before bad habits become too ingrained.

Rule 1: Top to Bottom
The first general rule is starting at the top and working down. This applies to both individual strokes, which are written from the top downwards, and with parts of a character such as the two parts of the character 哥 meaning *brother*. In short, begin with the topmost stroke.

Rule 2: Left to Right
When you encounter strokes that are not above or below each other, proceed from left to right. Again, this applies to individual strokes, which should be written from left to right but also to parts of the character, with radicals on the left written before the radicals on the right. An example of this can be seen in this character 如 which combines 女 for *woman* with 口 for *mouth*.

Rule 3: Horizontal before Vertical

In a character with horizontal and vertical crossing lines, such as 十, meaning *ten*, the horizontal line should be written first.

Rule 4: Down-to-the-Left before Down-to-the-Right

In a character with strokes which cross diagonally, the stroke going down and to the left should be written before the stroke going down and to the right, such as in the character 文 meaning *culture* or *language*.

Rule 5: Build the Box before Putting Stuff in It

Some characters are surrounded by a box. For example, the character 国, representing *country* or *kingdom*. In situations like this, the top and sides should be written before the middle, then the box should be closed on the bottom with the last stroke.

Rule 6: Minor Strokes Last

Characters often have dots or smaller strokes which are written last. The character for *small*, 小, is in this book. In this case, because the strokes on each side are much smaller, the center line is actually first, followed by the two on the outside.

田 tián

This character simply looks like a *field*. When 田 is combined with *earth*, 土, you get 里, which refers to a *small town* or *village*.

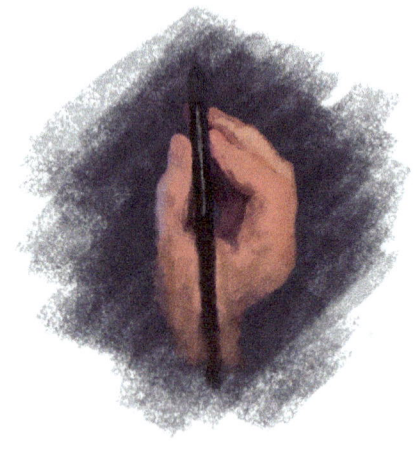

小 xiǎo

Imagine two fingers holding a small object to give this character its meaning of *small* or *little*. Take 小 and add the character for *eat*, 吃, and you get 小吃, meaning *snacks*.

女 nǚ

A representation of a woman. When we combine 女 with the character for *horse,* 马, we get a symbol that sounds like 马, but also refers to a woman: 妈. A character referring to a woman that sounds like 马? Mother!

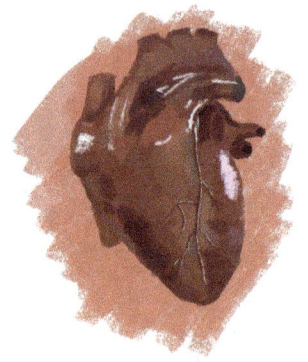

 xīn

心 is a stylized version of a *heart*. It may not look like a heart to many people, but does the ♥ symbol we use in the West seem any more accurate? This character is often used to express emotion, appearing in both the traditional character for *love*, 愛, and the character 恨, meaning *hate*.

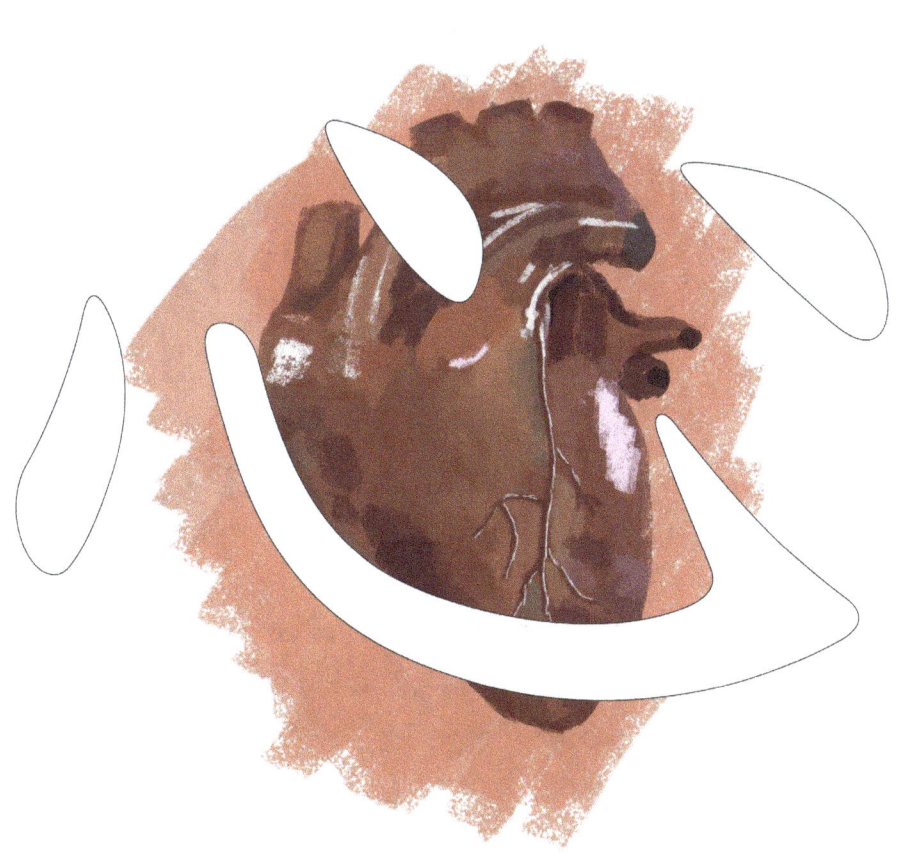

弓 gōng

A pictograph of a curved *bow*. When combined with 身, meaning *body*, you get the character 躬, the verb to bend the body, "to bow," similar to English in meaning: when the body bends like a curved bow, it bows.

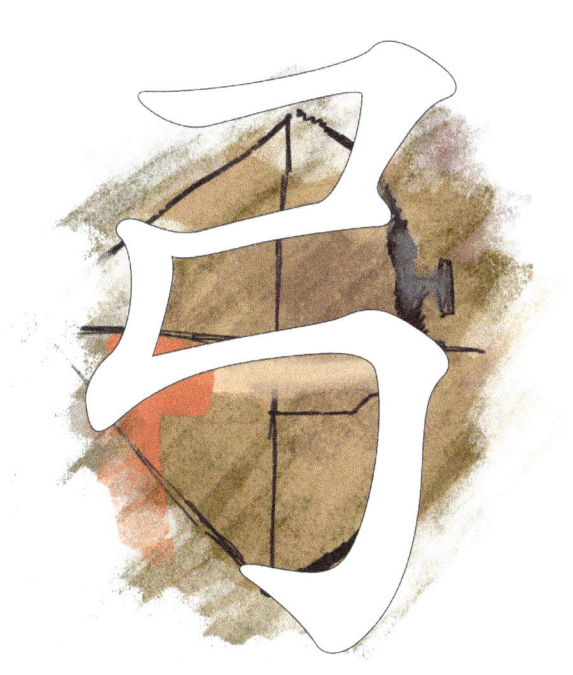

马 mǎ

Representing a *horse* rearing back, 马 can often be seen as a phonetic portion of a character. When combined with the character 女 (also seen in this book,) we get the character 妈, meaning *mother* which uses the same phonetic sound as 马.

大 dà

For the character 大, imagine someone with their arms spread wide. 大 means *big* or *large*. For instance, the term 大学, literally translated as "large school," means *university*.

The pictograph of a tree, 木, is by extension taken to mean *wood*. This is a very common radical, often in characters representing trees, such as 松, or *pine*, but also for objects made of wood. The radical for *wood*, 木, is combined with the radical for *container*, 匡, and becomes 框, or a *frame*.

水 shuǐ

The character for *water*, 水, often changes form when used in conjuction with other radicals. In the character 泉, which means *spring*, it remains basically the same. When we *wrap*, 包, something in *water*, 水, we get 泡, meaning *bubbles*. This is the most common alternate form of the water radical.

沐 mù

Remember that the character for *water*, 水, often changes form when used in a new character to 氵. This water radical is combined with 木 which in this case serves as a phonetic reminder of how the character is spoken. A character that sounds like 木 "mu" but has something to do with water becomes 沐, meaning *to wash* or *shampoo*.

尖 jiān

尖 ideographically combines the character 小 for *small* and 大 for *large* to represent something smaller on top and larger at the bottom, meaning *sharp*.

森　sēn

Assembling three 木 radicals which are pictographs of trees, we get 森, meaning *forest*. This is a very basic example of combining pictographs to create a new character.

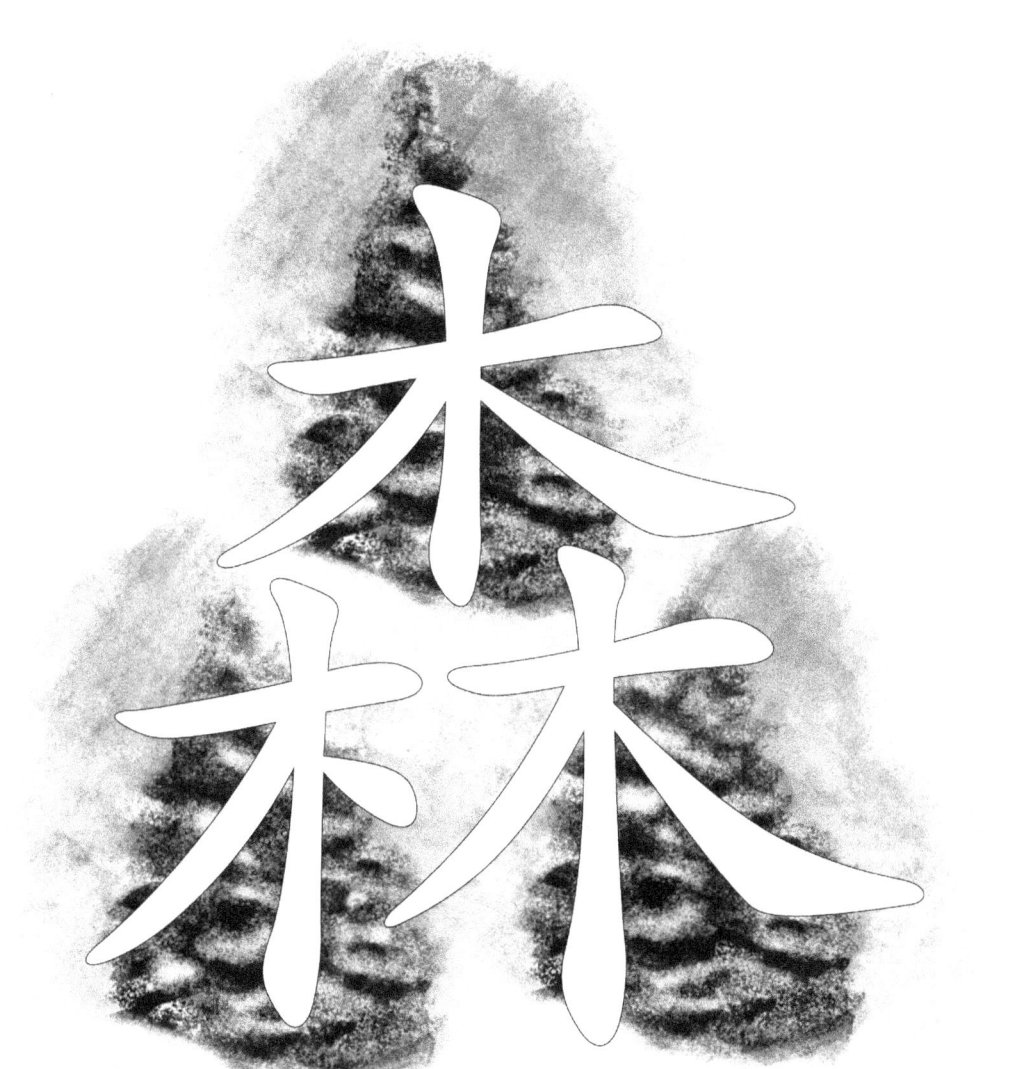

www.ingramcontent.com/pod-product-compliance
Lightning Source LLC
Chambersburg PA
CBHW051354070526
44584CB00025B/3767